# ARTIST TRANSCRIPTIONS
# KENNY G
## A HOLIDAY ALBUM

KENNY G

*Faith*

A HOLIDAY ALBUM

Photography: Patrick Demarcheller

ISBN 978-0-634-03061-1

HAL•LEONARD®
CORPORATION
7777 W. BLUEMOUND RD. P.O. BOX 13819 MILWAUKEE, WI 53213

Visit Hal Leonard Online at
www.halleonard.com

# Let It Snow! Let It Snow! Let It Snow!

Words by Sammy Cahn
Music by Jule Styne

Bb SOPRANO SAXOPHONE

Moderately (♩ = 124)

**B♭ Soprano Saxophone**

# The First Noël

Arranged by Walter Afanasieff

**B♭ SOPRANO SAXOPHONE**

Bb Soprano Saxophone

# I'll Be Home for Christmas

Words and Music by Kim Gannon and Walter Kent

Bb TENOR SAXOPHONE

**B♭ Tenor Saxophone**

# Sleigh Ride

Music by Leroy Anderson

**B♭ SOPRANO SAXOPHONE**

**B♭ Soprano Saxophone**

12

**B♭ Soprano Saxophone**

13

**B♭ Soprano Saxophone**

**B♭ Soprano Saxophone**

**B♭ Soprano Saxophone**

# The Christmas Song
## (Chestnuts Roasting on an Open Fire)

Music and Lyric by Mel Torme and Robert Wells

Bb SOPRANO SAXOPHONE

**Bb Soprano Saxophone**

# We Three Kings/Carol of the Bells

Arranged by Kenneth Gorelick and Walter Afanasieff

**B♭ SOPRANO SAXOPHONE**

Moderately (♩=160)

**B♭ Soprano Saxophone**

**B♭ Soprano Saxophone**

**B♭ Soprano Saxophone**

# O Christmas Tree

Arranged by Kenneth Gorelick and Walter Afanasieff

**Bb SOPRANO SAXOPHONE**

# Santa Claus Is Comin' to Town

Words by Haven Gillespie
Music by J. Fred Coots

**B♭ TENOR SAXOPHONE**

24

**B♭ Tenor Saxophone**

**B♭ Tenor Saxophone**

# Eternal Light

Arranged by Kenneth Gorelick and Walter Afanasieff

**B♭ SOPRANO SAXOPHONE**

# Ave Maria

Arranged by Kenneth Gorelick and Walter Afanasieff

**Bb SOPRANO SAXOPHONE**

**B♭ Soprano Saxophone**

**Bb Soprano Saxophone**

# Auld Lang Syne

Arranged by Kenneth Gorelick and Walter Afanasieff

**B♭ SOPRANO SAXOPHONE**

**B♭ Soprano Saxophone**

# ARTIST TRANSCRIPTIONS

Artist Transcriptions are authentic, note-for-note transcriptions of today's hottest artists in jazz, pop and rock. These outstanding, accurate arrangements are in an easy-to-read format which includes all essential lines. Artist Transcriptions can be used to perform, sequence or for reference.

## FLUTE

| | | |
|---|---|---|
| 00672379 | Eric Dolphy Collection | $19.95 |
| 00672582 | The Very Best of James Galway | $19.99 |
| 00672372 | James Moody Collection – Sax and Flute | $19.95 |

## GUITAR & BASS

| | | |
|---|---|---|
| 00660113 | Guitar Style of George Benson | $19.99 |
| 00672573 | Ray Brown – Legendary Jazz Bassist | $22.99 |
| 00672331 | Ron Carter Collection | $24.99 |
| 00660115 | Al Di Meola – Friday Night in San Francisco | $22.99 |
| 00604043 | Al Di Meola – Music, Words, Pictures | $14.95 |
| 00125617 | Best of Herb Ellis | $19.99 |
| 00699306 | Jim Hall – Exploring Jazz Guitar | $19.99 |
| 00672353 | The Joe Pass Collection | $22.99 |
| 00673216 | John Patitucci | $19.99 |
| 00672374 | Johnny Smith – Guitar Solos | $24.99 |

## PIANO & KEYBOARD

| | | |
|---|---|---|
| 00672338 | The Monty Alexander Collection | $19.95 |
| 00672487 | Monty Alexander Plays Standards | $19.95 |
| 00672520 | Count Basie Collection | $19.95 |
| 00192307 | Bebop Piano Legends | $19.99 |
| 00113680 | Blues Piano Legends | $22.99 |
| 00672526 | The Bill Charlap Collection | $19.99 |
| 00278003 | A Charlie Brown Christmas | $19.99 |
| 00672300 | Chick Corea – Paint the World | $19.99 |
| 00146105 | Bill Evans – Alone | $19.99 |
| 00672548 | The Mastery of Bill Evans | $16.99 |
| 00672365 | Bill Evans – Play Standards | $22.99 |
| 00121885 | Bill Evans – Time Remembered | $19.99 |
| 00672510 | Bill Evans Trio Vol. 1: 1959-1961 | $29.99 |
| 00672511 | Bill Evans Trio Vol. 2: 1962-1965 | $27.99 |
| 00672512 | Bill Evans Trio Vol. 3: 1968-1974 | $29.99 |
| 00672513 | Bill Evans Trio Vol. 4: 1979-1980 | $24.95 |
| 00193332 | Erroll Garner – Concert by the Sea | $22.99 |
| 00672486 | Vince Guaraldi Collection | $19.99 |
| 00289644 | The Definitive Vince Guaraldi | $34.99 |
| 00672419 | Herbie Hancock Collection | $22.99 |
| 00672438 | Hampton Hawes Collection | $19.95 |
| 00672322 | Ahmad Jamal Collection | $27.99 |
| 00255671 | Jazz Piano Masterpieces | $22.99 |
| 00124367 | Jazz Piano Masters Play Rodgers & Hammerstein | $19.99 |
| 00672564 | Best of Jeff Lorber | $19.99 |

| | | |
|---|---|---|
| 00672476 | Brad Mehldau Collection | $24.99 |
| 00672388 | Best of Thelonious Monk | $22.99 |
| 00672389 | Thelonious Monk Collection | $24.99 |
| 00672390 | Thelonious Monk Plays Jazz Standards – Volume 1 | $22.99 |
| 00672391 | Thelonious Monk Plays Jazz Standards – Volume 2 | $24.99 |
| 00672433 | Jelly Roll Morton – The Piano Rolls | $19.99 |
| 00672553 | Charlie Parker Piano featuring The Paul Smith Trio (Book/CD) | $19.95 |
| 00264094 | Oscar Peterson – Night Train | $19.99 |
| 00672544 | Oscar Peterson – Originals | $14.99 |
| 00672531 | Oscar Peterson – Plays Duke Ellington | $27.99 |
| 00672563 | Oscar Peterson – A Royal Wedding Suite | $19.99 |
| 00672569 | Oscar Peterson – Tracks | $19.99 |
| 00672533 | Oscar Peterson – Trios | $29.99 |
| 00672534 | Very Best of Oscar Peterson | $27.99 |
| 00672371 | Bud Powell Classics | $22.99 |
| 00672376 | Bud Powell Collection | $24.99 |
| 00672507 | Gonzalo Rubalcaba Collection | $19.95 |
| 00672303 | Horace Silver Collection | $24.99 |
| 00672316 | Art Tatum Collection | $24.99 |
| 00672355 | Art Tatum Solo Book | $22.99 |
| 00672357 | The Billy Taylor Collection | $24.95 |
| 00673215 | McCoy Tyner | $22.99 |
| 00672321 | Cedar Walton Collection | $19.95 |
| 00672519 | Kenny Werner Collection | $19.95 |

## SAXOPHONE

| | | |
|---|---|---|
| 00672566 | The Mindi Abair Collection | $14.99 |
| 00673244 | Julian "Cannonball" Adderley Collection | $22.99 |
| 00673237 | Michael Brecker | $24.99 |
| 00672429 | Michael Brecker Collection | $24.99 |
| 00672394 | James Carter Collection | $19.95 |
| 00672529 | John Coltrane – Giant Steps | $17.99 |
| 00672494 | John Coltrane – A Love Supreme | $17.99 |
| 00672493 | John Coltrane Plays "Coltrane Changes" | $19.95 |
| 00672453 | John Coltrane Plays Standards | $24.99 |
| 00673233 | John Coltrane Solos | $29.99 |
| 00672328 | Paul Desmond Collection | $22.99 |
| 00672530 | Kenny Garrett Collection | $24.99 |
| 00699375 | Stan Getz | $19.99 |
| 00672377 | Stan Getz – Bossa Novas | $24.99 |
| 00673254 | Great Tenor Sax Solos | $22.99 |

| | | |
|---|---|---|
| 00672523 | Coleman Hawkins Collection | $24.99 |
| 00672330 | Best of Joe Henderson | $24.99 |
| 00673239 | Best of Kenny G | $22.99 |
| 00673229 | Kenny G – Breathless | $19.99 |
| 00672462 | Kenny G – Classics in the Key of G | $24.99 |
| 00672485 | Kenny G – Faith: A Holiday Album | $17.99 |
| 00672373 | Kenny G – The Moment | $22.99 |
| 00672498 | Jackie McLean Collection | $19.95 |
| 00672372 | James Moody Collection – Sax and Flute | $19.95 |
| 00672416 | Frank Morgan Collection | $19.95 |
| 00672539 | Gerry Mulligan Collection | $24.99 |
| 00672561 | Best of Sonny Rollins | $22.99 |
| 00102751 | Sonny Rollins, Art Blakey & Kenny Drew with the Modern Jazz Quartet | $17.99 |
| 00675000 | David Sanborn Collection | $19.99 |
| 00672528 | The Bud Shank Collection | $19.95 |
| 00672491 | The New Best of Wayne Shorter | $24.99 |
| 00672550 | The Sonny Stitt Collection | $19.95 |
| 00672524 | Lester Young Collection | $22.99 |

## TROMBONE

| | | |
|---|---|---|
| 00672332 | J.J. Johnson Collection | $24.99 |
| 00672489 | Steve Turré Collection | $19.99 |

## TRUMPET

| | | |
|---|---|---|
| 00672557 | Herb Alpert Collection | $19.99 |
| 00672480 | Louis Armstrong Collection | $19.99 |
| 00672481 | Louis Armstrong Plays Standards | $19.99 |
| 00672435 | Chet Baker Collection | $24.99 |
| 00672556 | Best of Chris Botti | $19.99 |
| 00672448 | Miles Davis – Originals, Vol. 1 | $19.99 |
| 00672451 | Miles Davis – Originals, Vol. 2 | $19.95 |
| 00672449 | Miles Davis – Standards, Vol. 2 | $19.95 |
| 00672479 | Dizzy Gillespie Collection | $19.95 |
| 00673214 | Freddie Hubbard | $19.99 |
| 00672506 | Chuck Mangione Collection | $22.99 |
| 00672525 | Arturo Sandoval – Trumpet Evolution | $19.99 |

HAL•LEONARD®

Visit our web site for songlists or to order online from your favorite music retailer at
**www.halleonard.com**

Prices, content, and availability subject to change without notice.